DREAMY COTTAGES

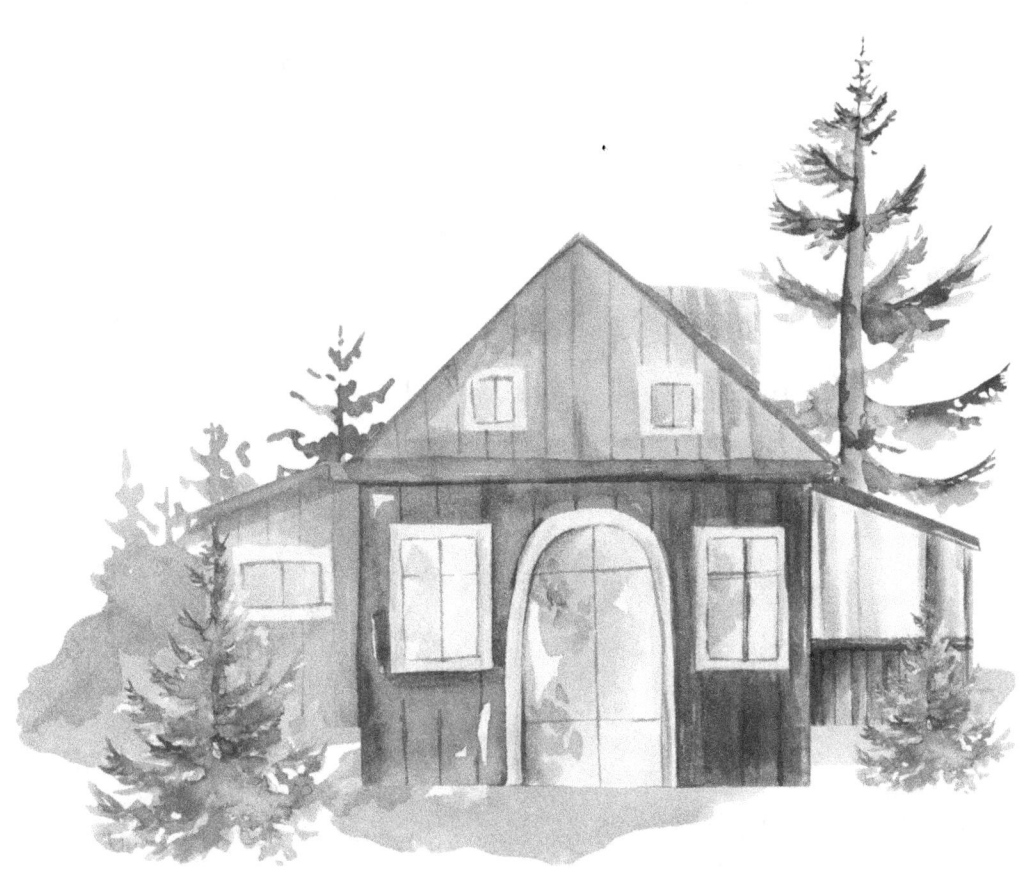

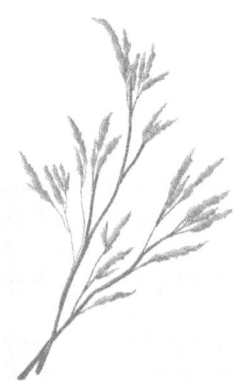

Welcome...

Whether you're seeking a tranquil interlude in a hectic day, igniting your creative spark, or just savoring the art of coloring, these charming scenes crafted by skilled artists are meant to offer hours of relaxation and happiness.

Keep in mind, there's no prescribed way to color these drawings. You're encouraged to play with different hues, textures, and approaches. Allow your imagination to run wild, but above all, make sure to enjoy the process!

MOORE'S
PUBLISHING

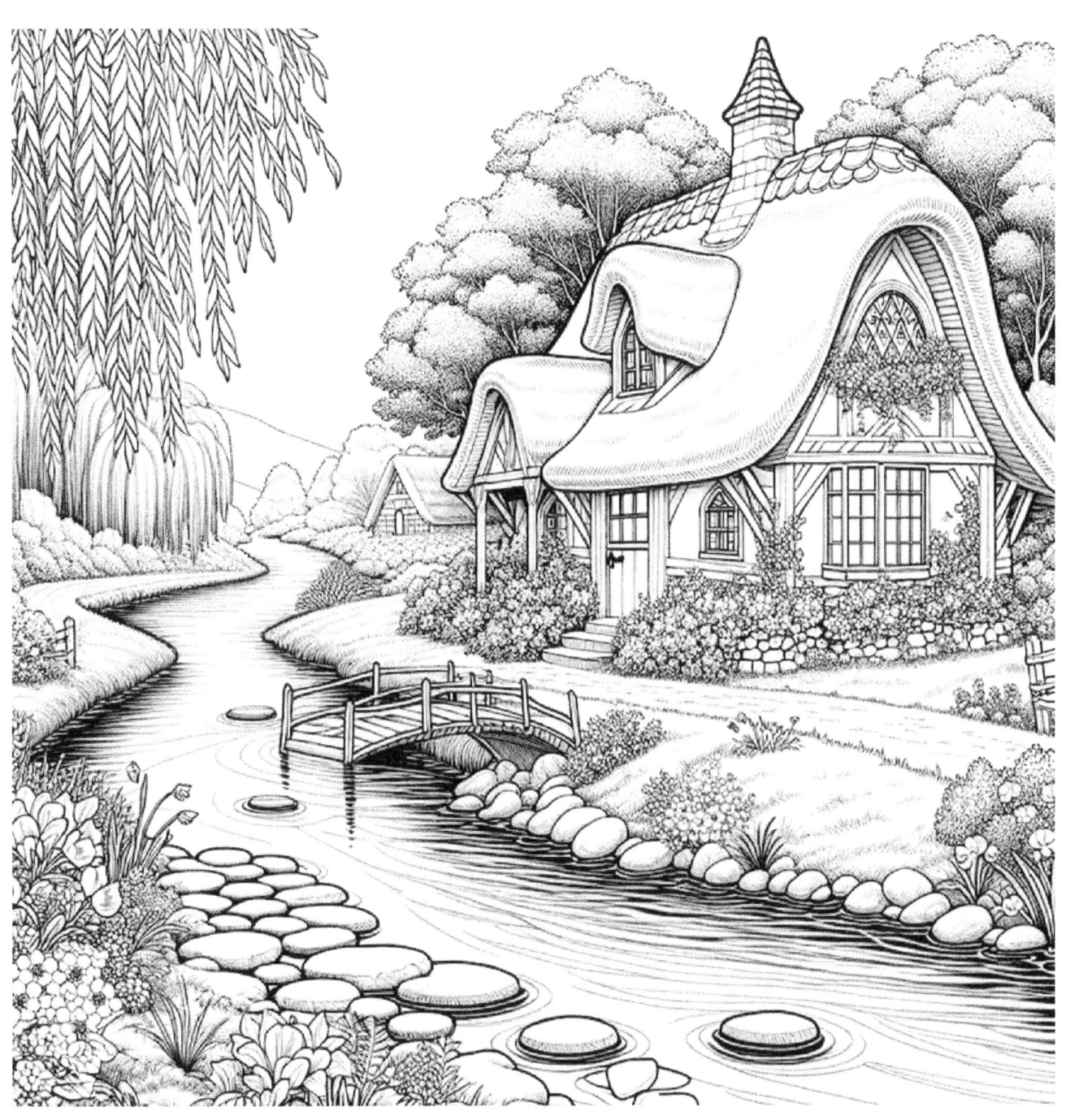

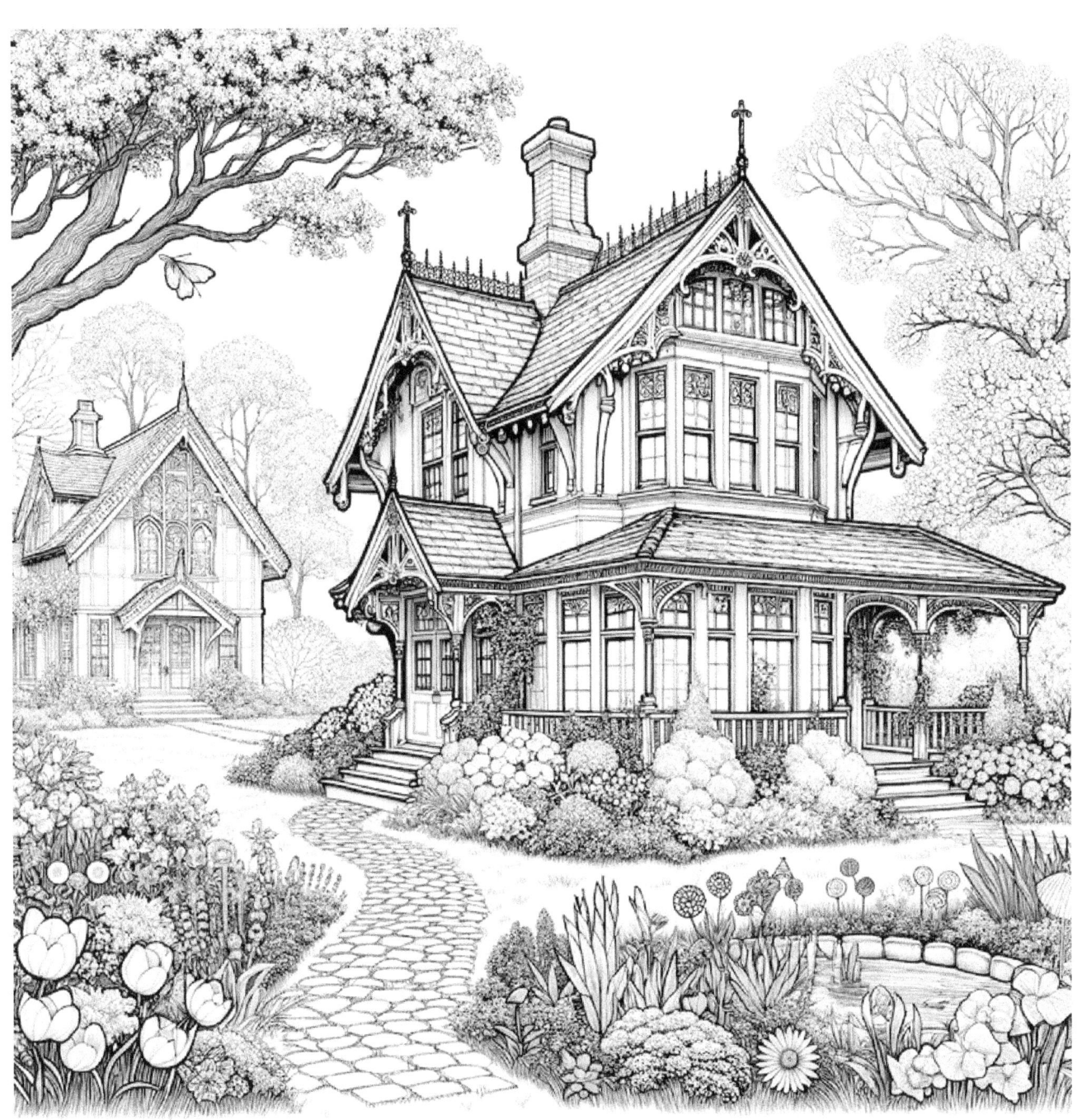

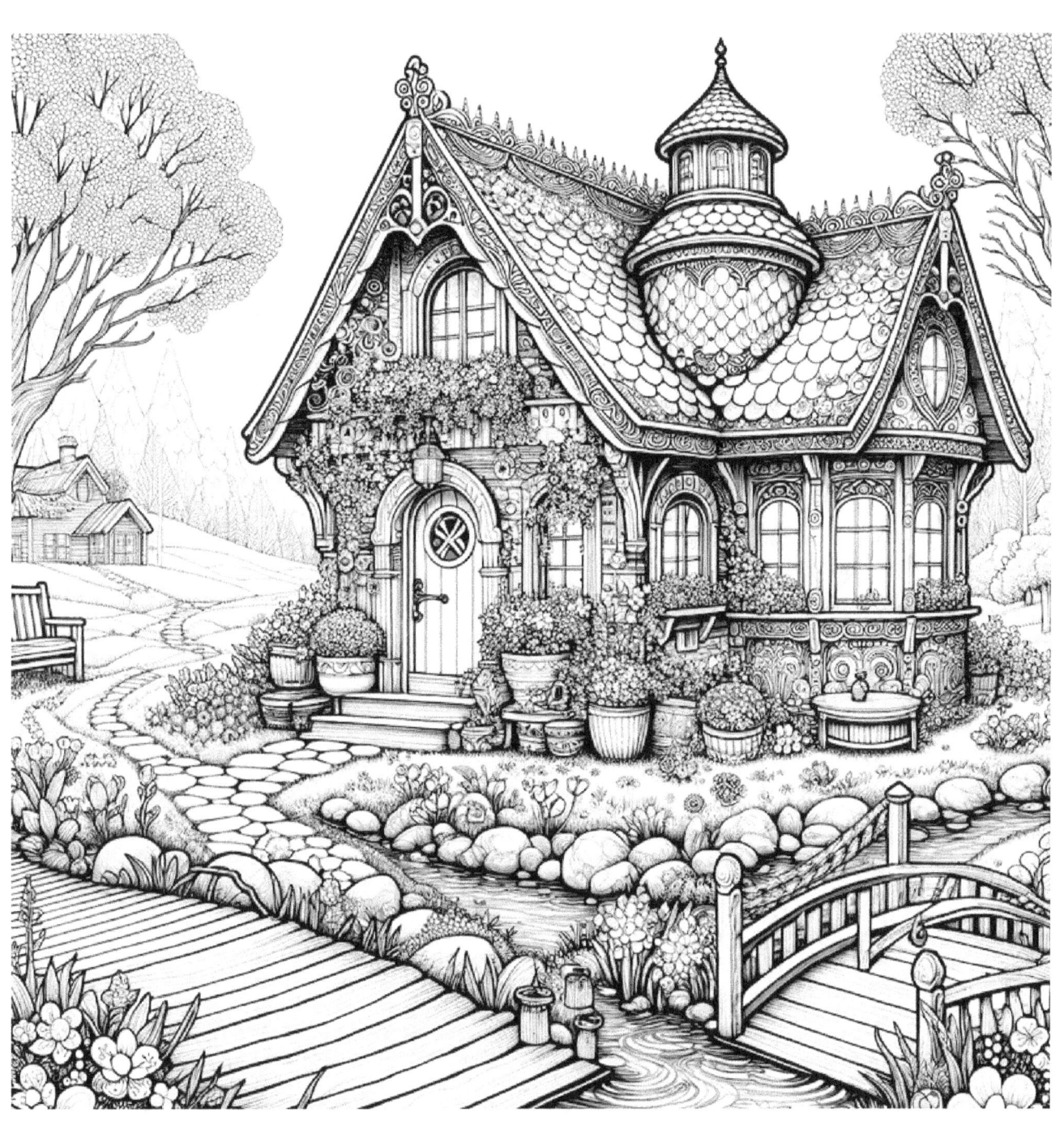

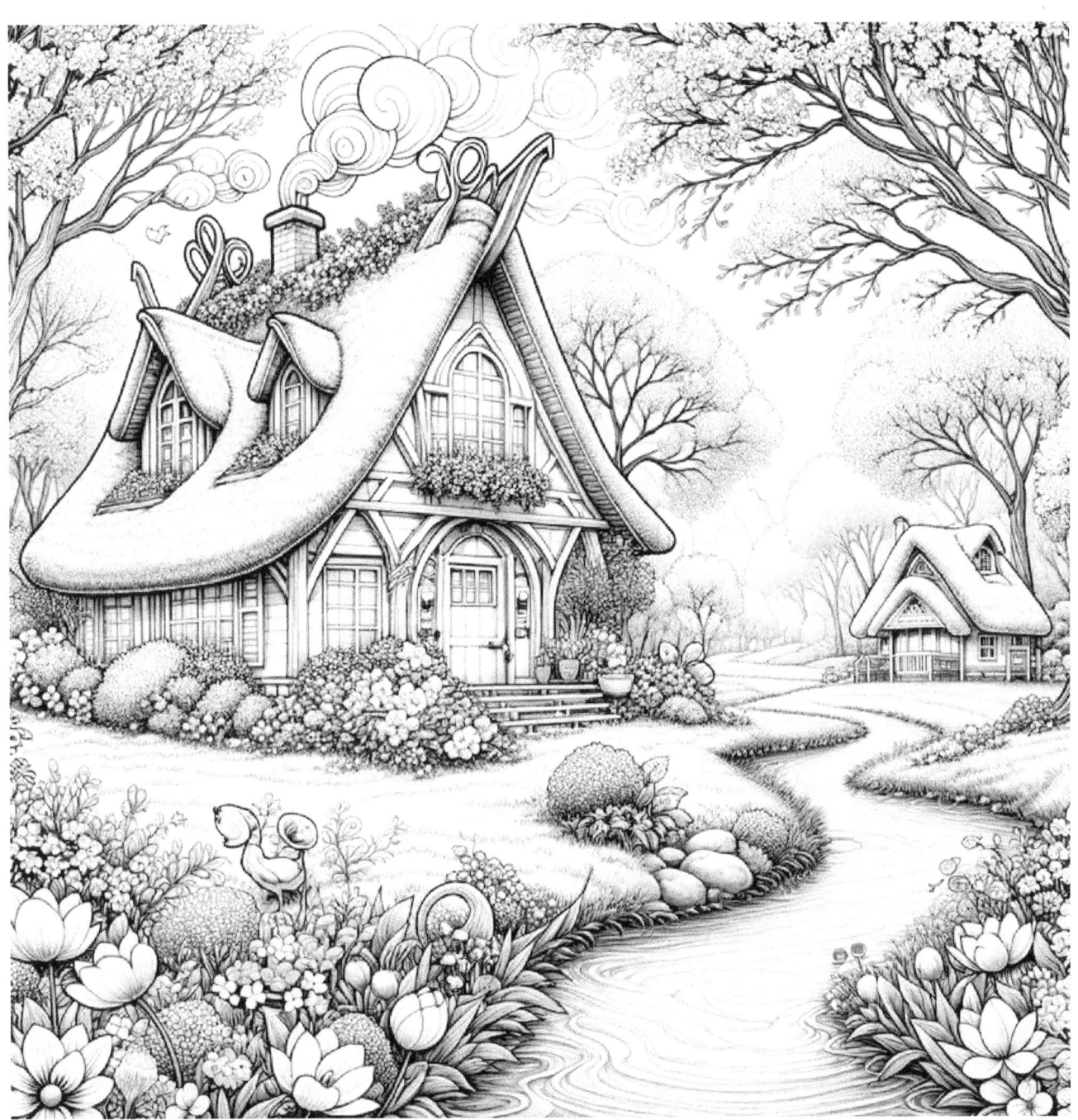

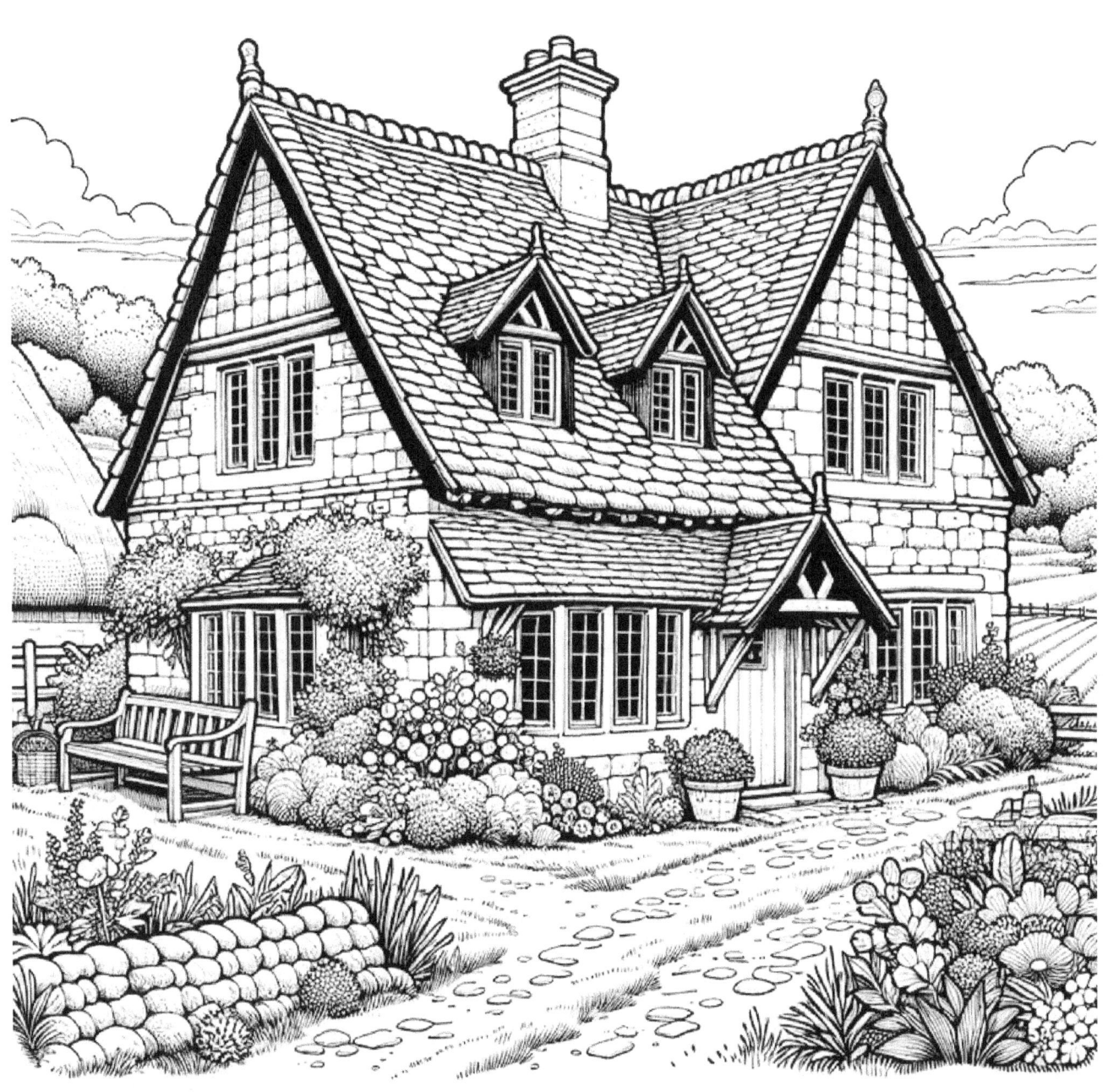

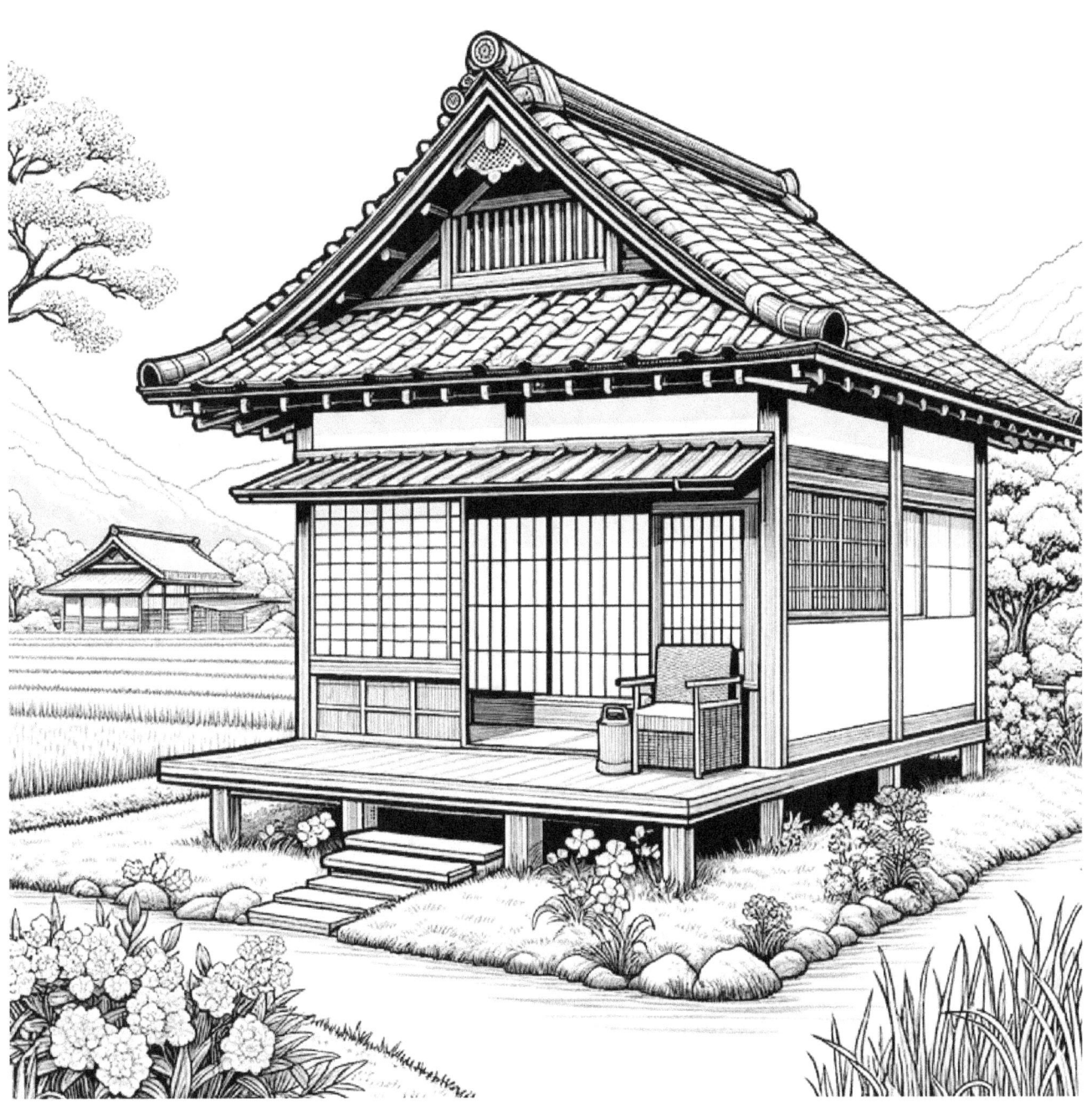

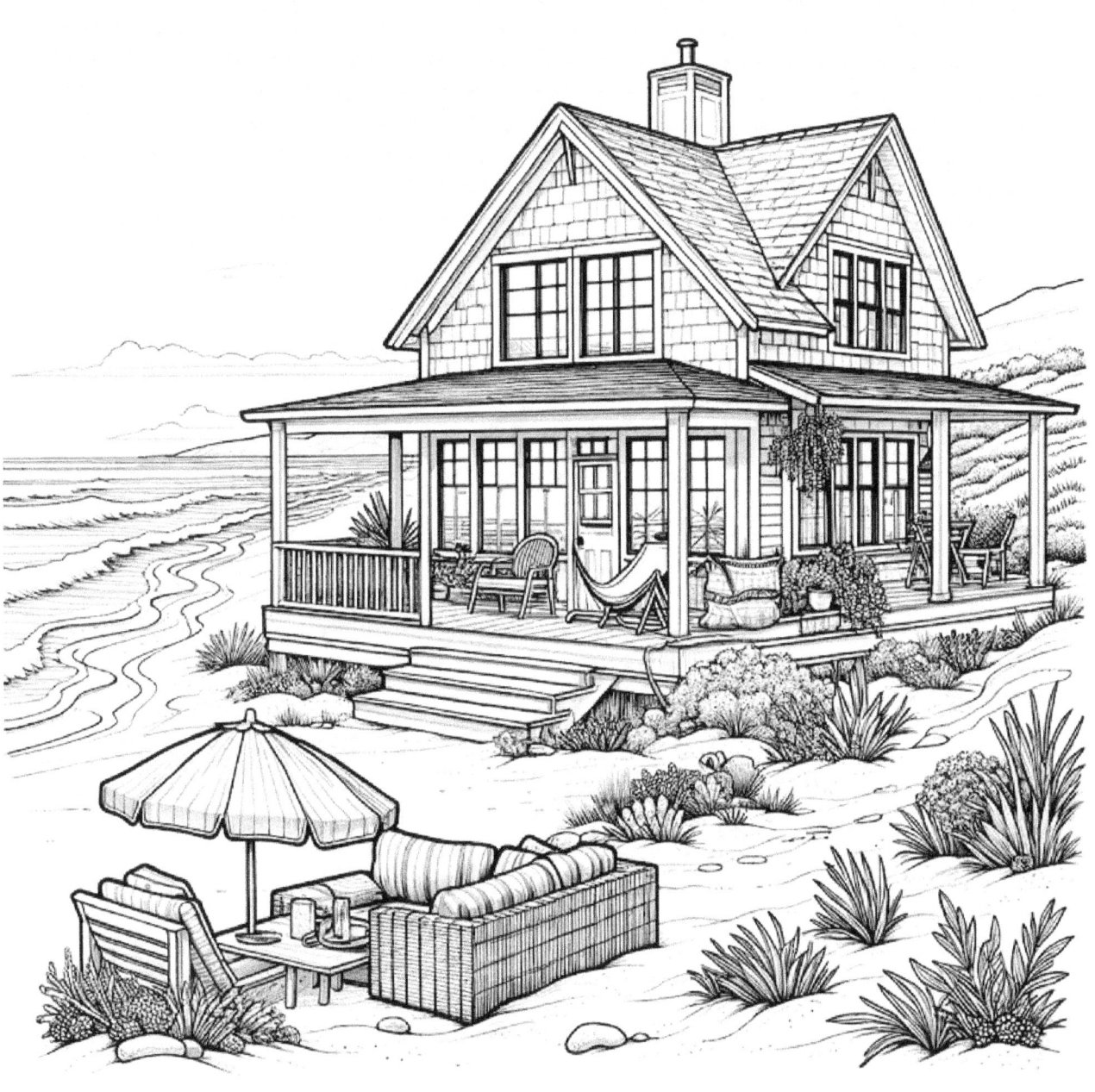

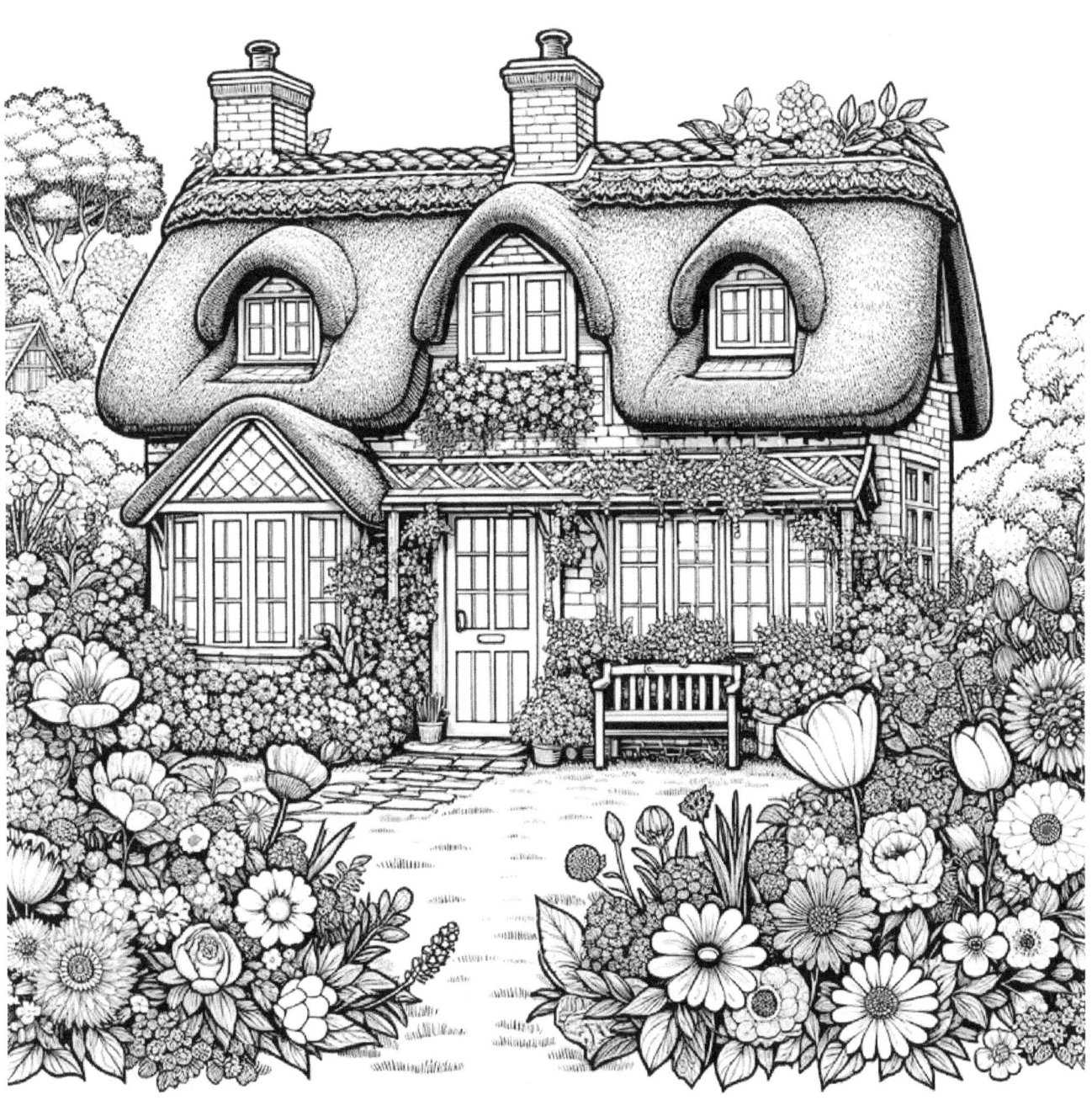

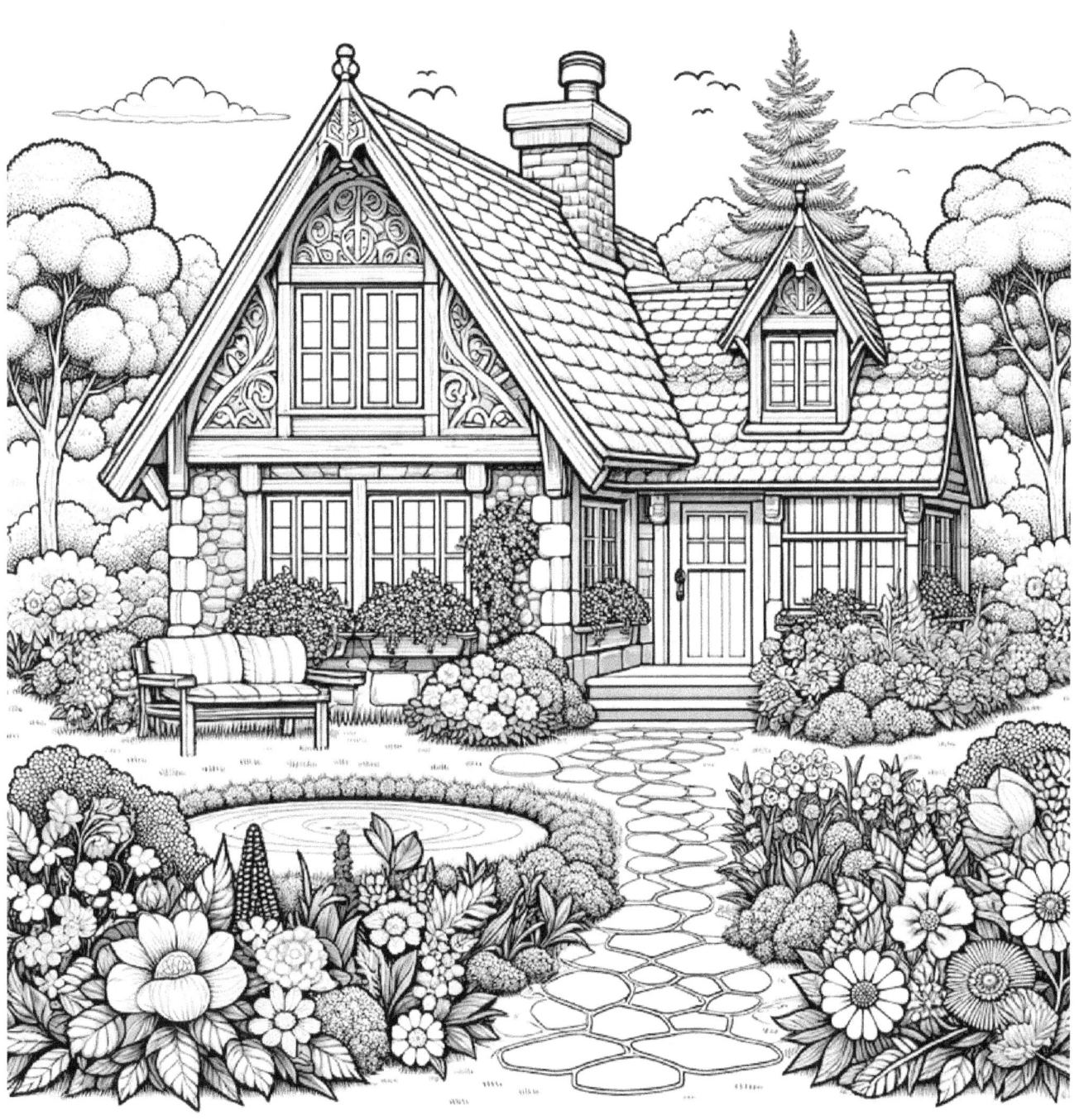

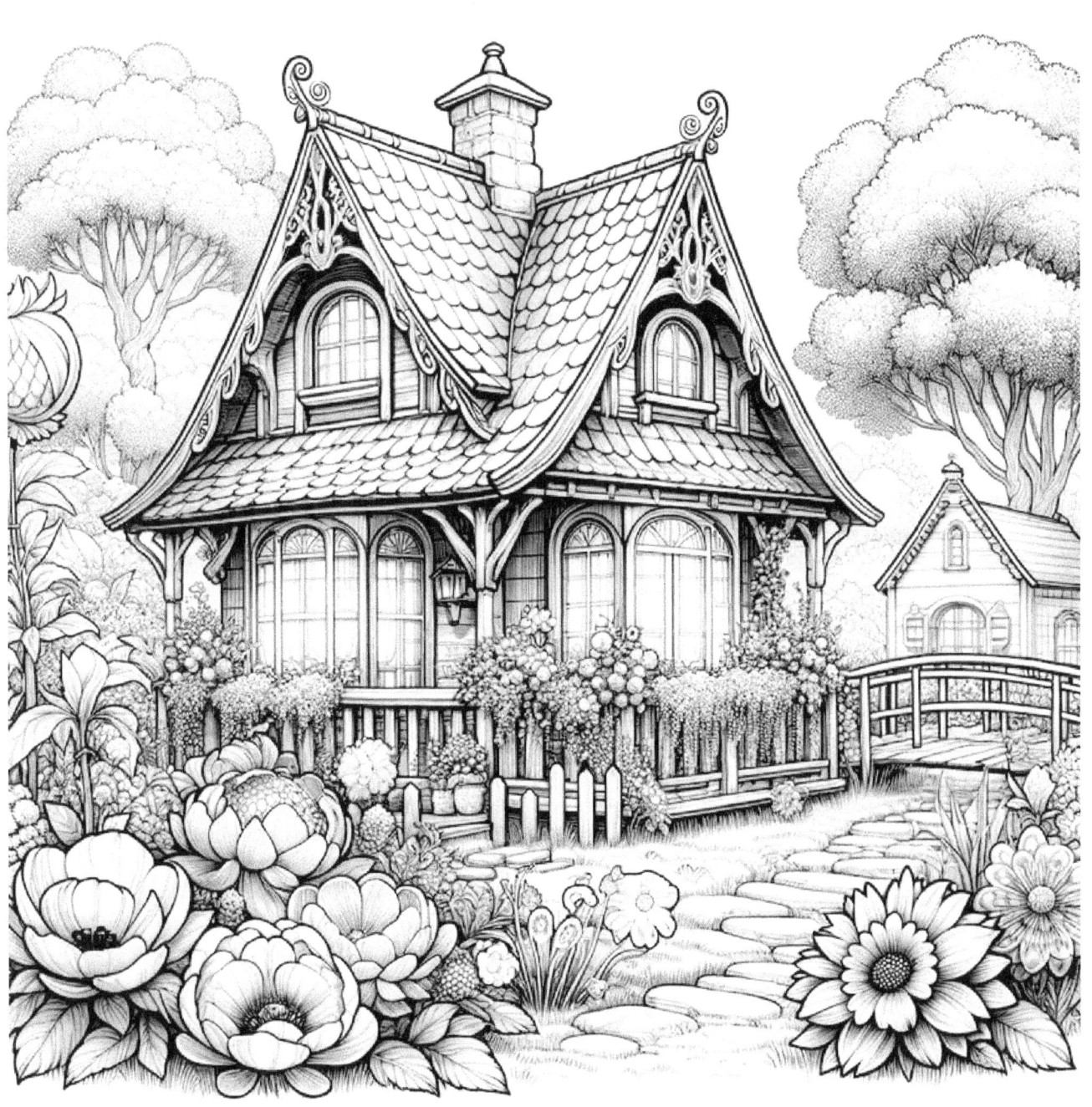

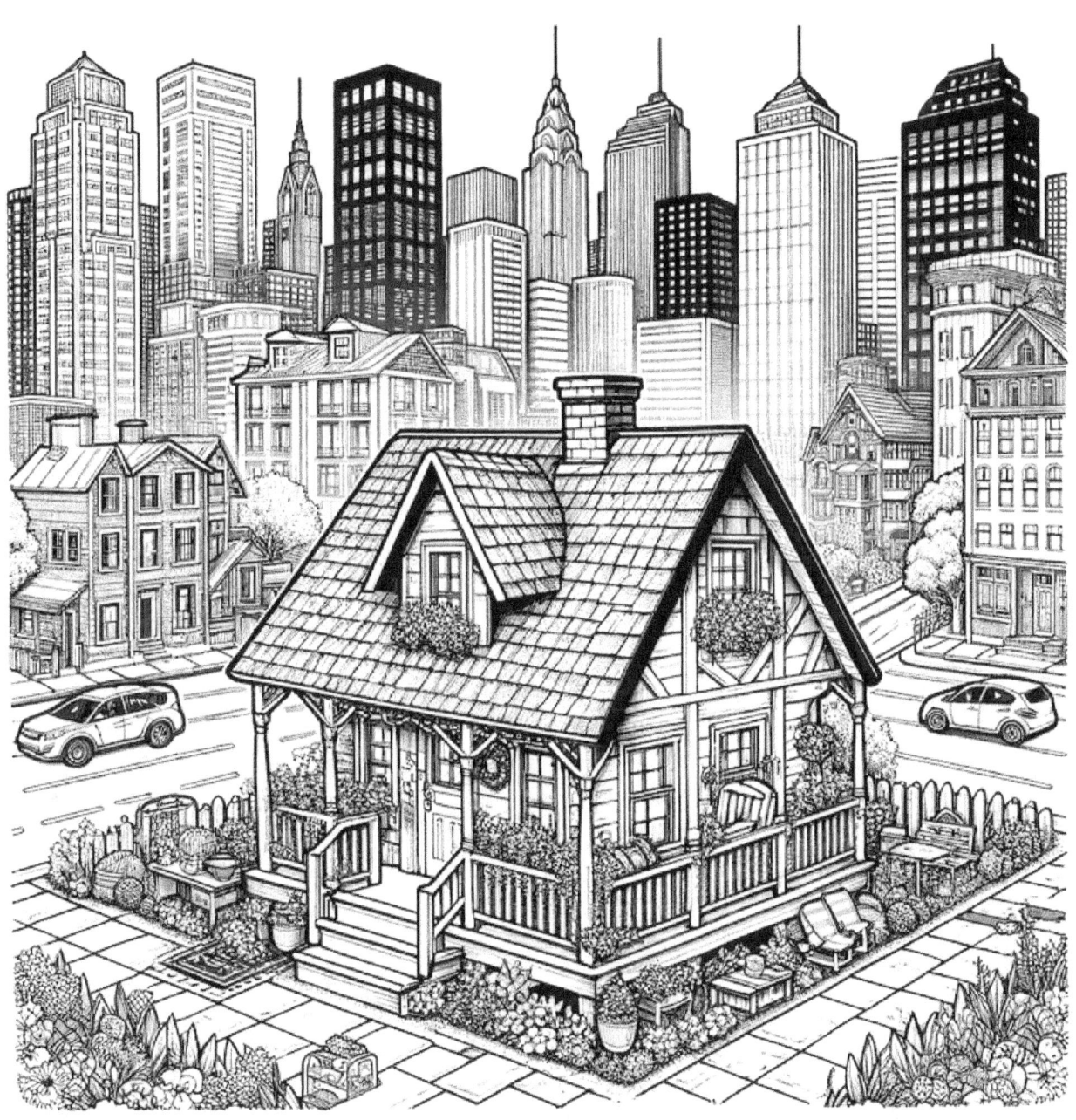

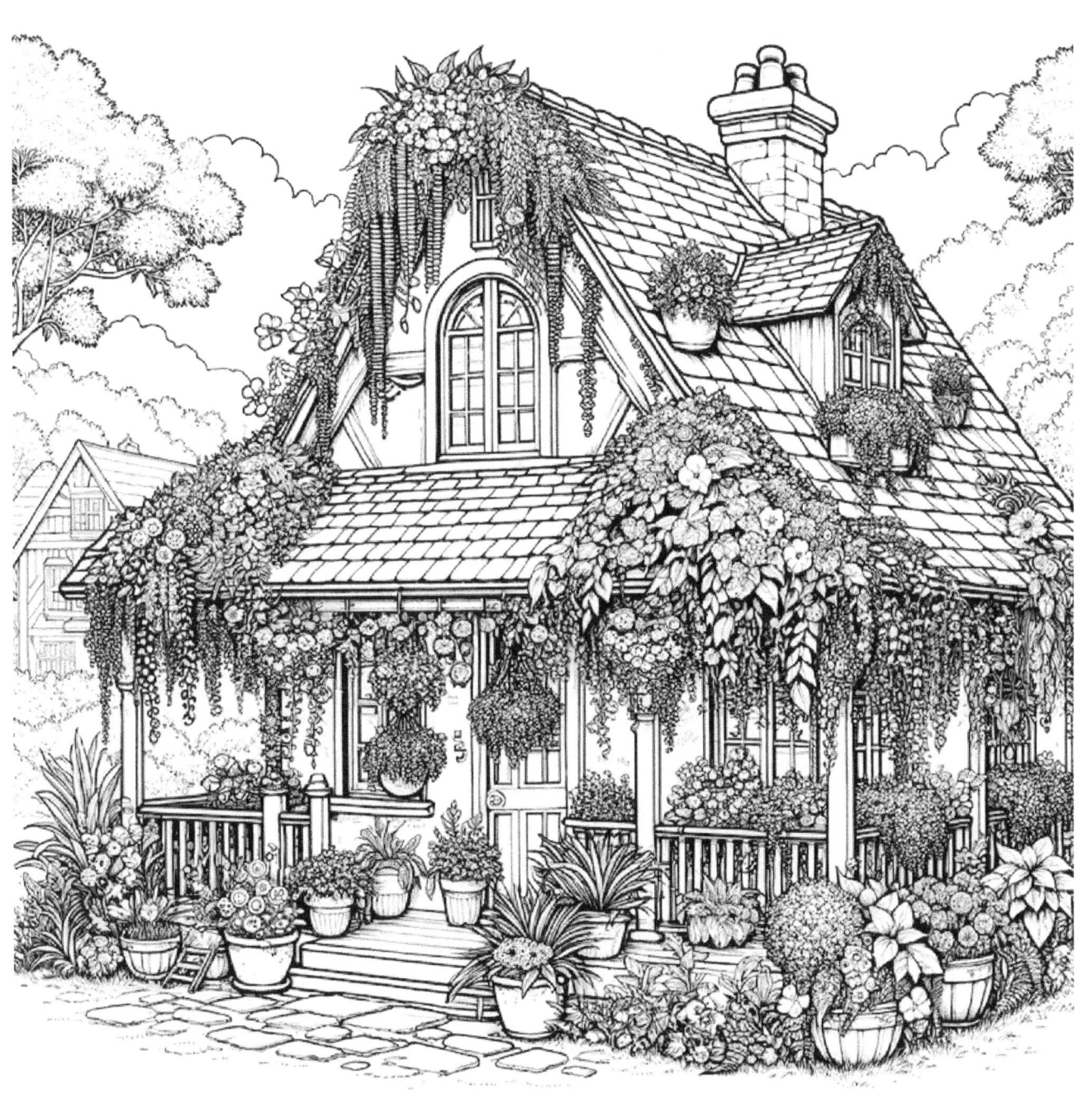

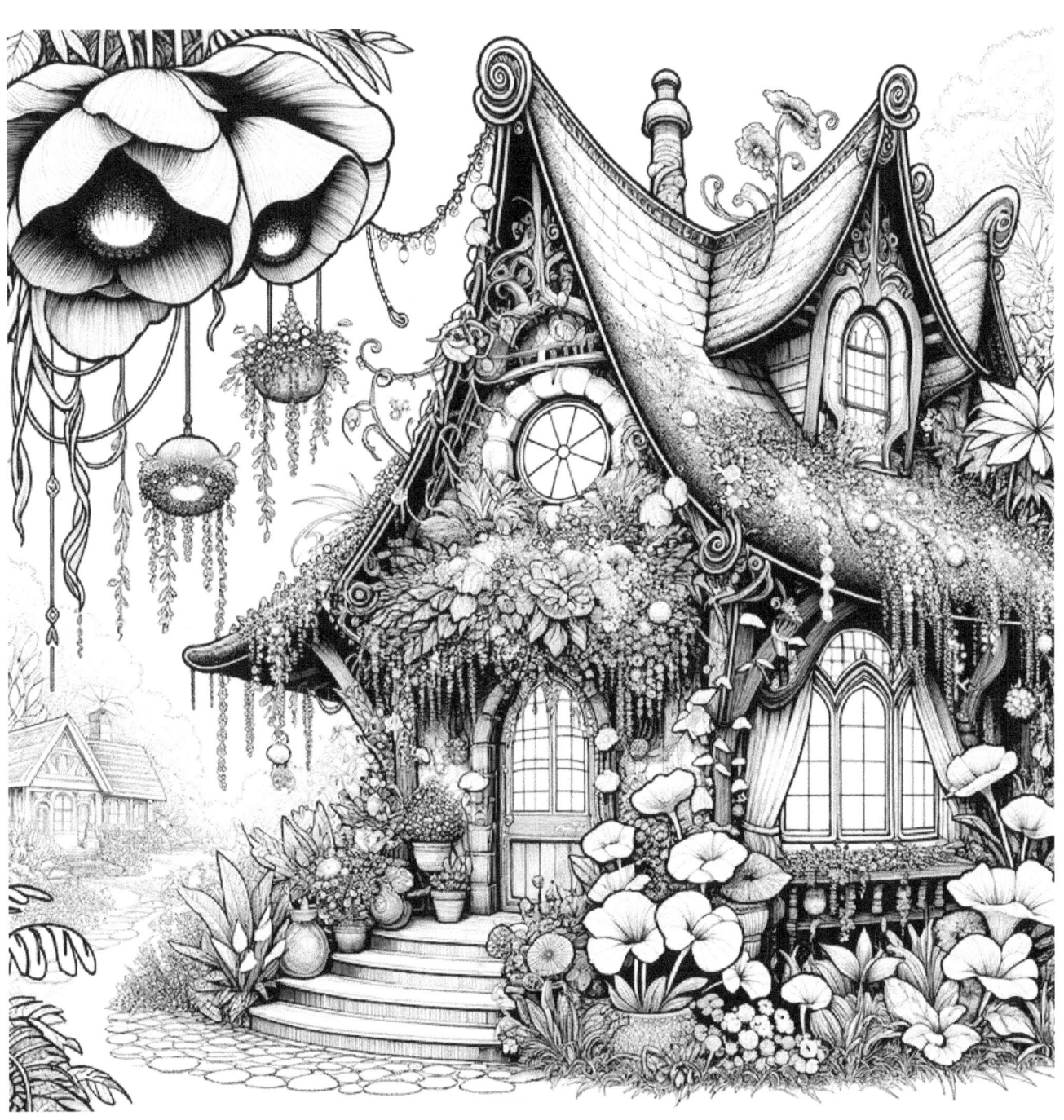

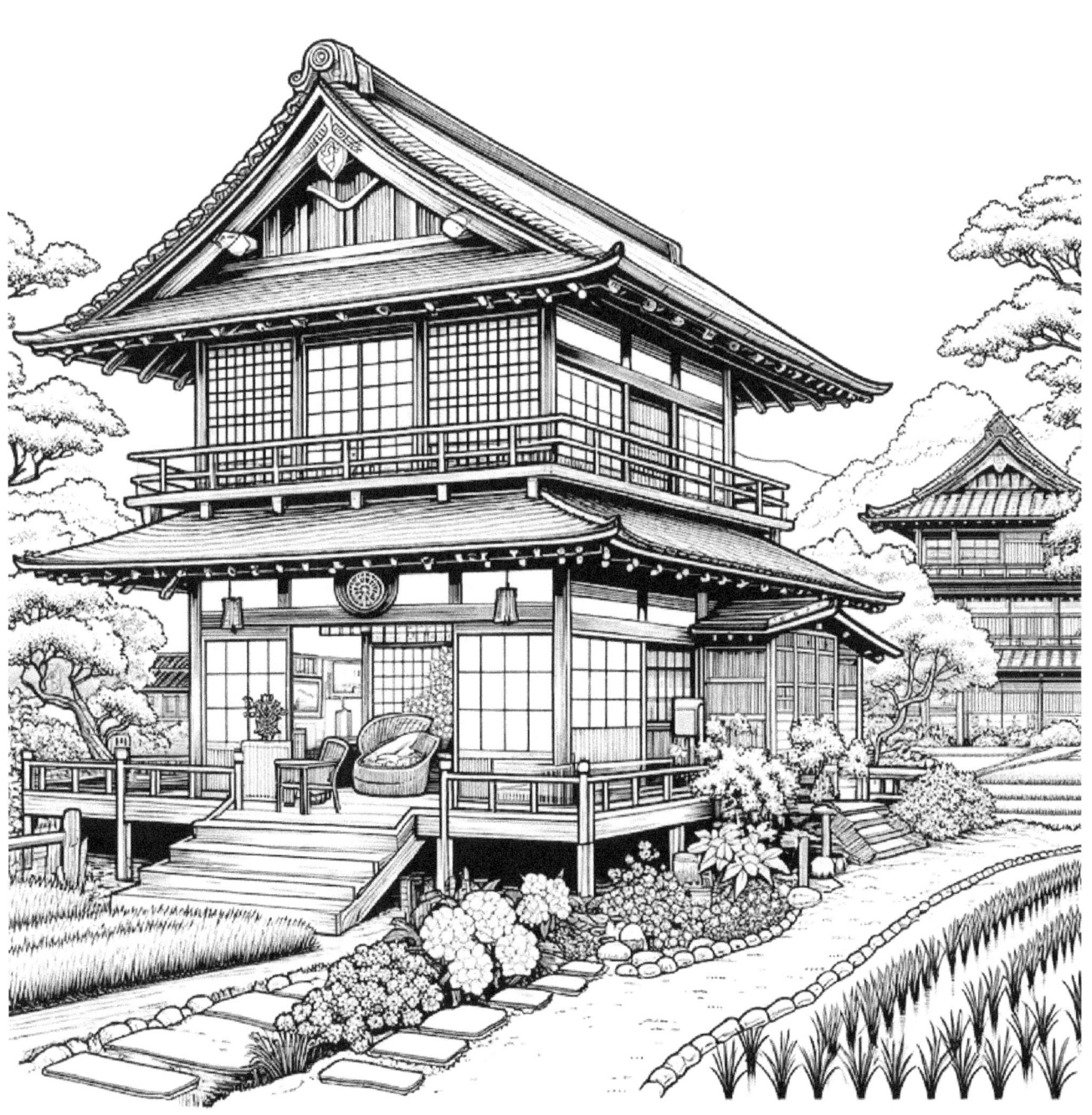

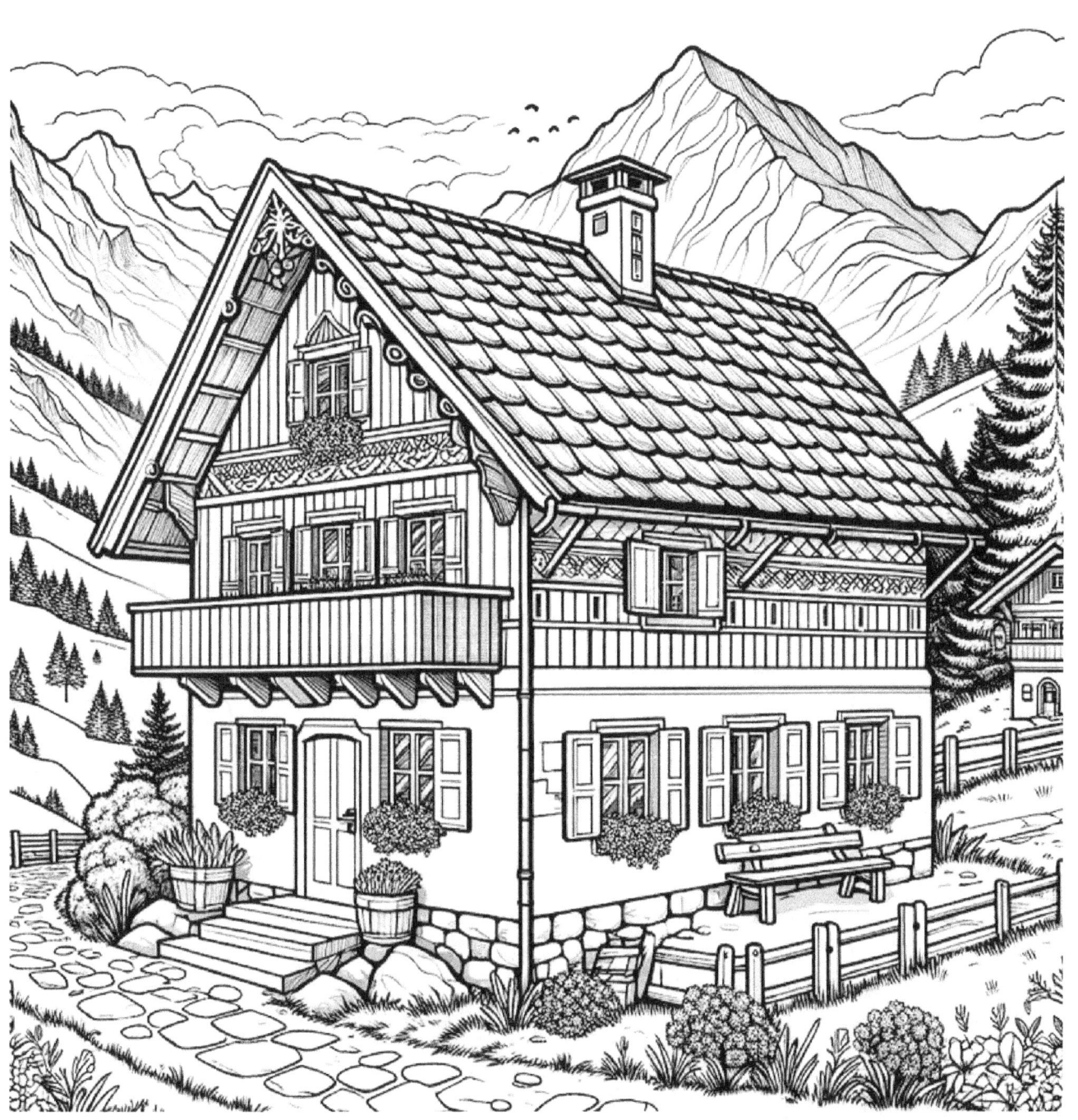

www.ingramcontent.com/pod-product-compliance
Lightning Source LLC
Chambersburg PA
CBHW080938290526
45795CB00007BA/2811